Praise for
Catastrophic Molting

"Creation is a necessary endeavor," Amy Shimshon-Santo reminds us, and *Catastrophic Molting* is a necessary book. These poems thrum with anger ("who can be witness/to these times/and not want to be thunder?") and glow with compassion. Her poems are awake to both the pain and beauty of our world. At the end of the title poem, she asks "what if we were a part of a whole/that loved us without ceasing?" Being inside this book feels like being part of such a whole, an immersive ocean of unceasing love.

—Gayle Brandeis

Amy Shimshon-Santo's *Catastrophic Molting* is an exploration of the deeper connections we inhabit. The poems weave the tragedies we experience daily with the beauty and wonderment of being alive, "I began to see/how the world is/all things linked/in the same place." Among separation and closeness, desperation and hope, she invites us to thrive in the abundance that is all around us.

—Leonora Simonovis

In *Catastrophic Molting* Amy Shimshon-Santo's poems of revelation are made in an age of streaming messages, zooming interactions, war, the police state, incarceration, and toxic cities. Her poems are a space to heal our cuerpos with her dazzling butterfly wisdom, and sky warrior rhymes.

—Adrian Ernesto Cepeda

Amy Shimshon-Santo's poems are the words of a survivor, a warrior, and a creator. Time and time again, across borders and languages, her writing takes us into sensuous and deeply emotional places, finding beauty and rootedness and meaning in everyday moments and extraordinary landscapes.

—Héctor Tobar

Amy Shimshon-Santo is the most organic poet I have ever read. Her art erupts or flows as the subject demands, cherishing and berating the world with equal ferocity; one minute politically exigent, the next dreamy and attuned to the language of the tiniest living thing.

—Mamle Kabu

Catastrophic Molting

FLOWERSONG
PRESS

by
Amy Shimshon-Santo

FLOWERSONG
PRESS

OTHER TITLES
BY AMY SHIMSHON-SANTO

Even the Milky Way is Undocumented

Endless Bowls of Sky

Catastrophic Molting

"If we are not capable of transforming the pain within ourselves, happiness would not be possible…If we learn to take good care of our suffering, we can help others do the same."

—*Thich Nhat Hanh*

declaration

whereas the galaxy deserves better,

whereas I am a mother who is the descendent of circumstances
beyond our control,

whereas I was born into a female body and have generated life,

whereas I am daughter, a granddaughter, a great granddaughter,

whereas the world is a spinning disc trying to unlock
mutual understanding,

whereas one must learn how to learn and keep learning
so as not to drown in ignorance,

whereas I am powerful,

I declare myself a living being,
aware and evolving,
prepared to face ugliness with a warrior's mindset,
imbued with the strength of health and wisdom.

so be it.

Contents

1 / Contagion

2 / Sangue

3 / Pelage

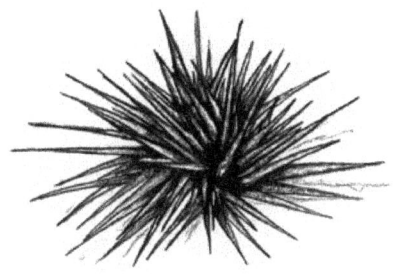

1 / CONTAGION

a green moth circled her eyes
thunder rumbled
wind came in, rocking back & forth

ENDLESS BOWLS OF SKY

- The poems in this first section, Contagion, are erasures written for the virus from pages in Ben Okri's novel The Famished Road.

1.

   beating, trembling
   mouth quivered
   one eye bruised
   cut in six places

   someone began to plead
   woman spoke
   of mercy
   — compassion

2.

   outside, birds fallen
   intense orange — molten
   people dressed in bright suits
   heavy, inescapable air
   come in my people, come in.

   afraid of tabletops and curtains
   too stunned to move, confused
   I picked time
   I held water
   I said nothing
   I held my hands and splinters

3.

   a table wobbled, man jumped
   from one table to another

don't worry, said the table
he didn't seem to notice
his shoes' horrible sweat

4.

a lantern rocked on the table,
fell and broke, calabashes
cracked open, smoke filled the air
screaming blue night

everything was burning
buckets of water poured
everywhere, on the tables and walls
glass and wood, sticking
she turned and lashed back
whipping the air, quick on her feet
she tore in several places at the same time
north south, west east
crackling with electric fury

the place was a mess
tables broken, crushed spoons
torn clothes and vomit on the floor
benches upside down

alone, surrounded by night
her hands trembled, she wept
swallowed, wiped her face

go find somewhere else
run, run! came a chorus
sweep away sorrows

she swayed, eyes opening
and shutting with the ecstasy
of a dark lantern

5.

    the forest walked
    in poor clothes, with hunger

    the facts of their lives
    stood outside

    trees can make life continue
    clustered, fast-changing
    sky, spread shadows
    on the burning earth

    people melted back
    I went inside,
    shut my eyes

    the forest will swallow you,
    then I will become a tree

6.

    silent, open eyes
    I heard water, birds
    calling outside

    space of peace, inside me
    soft voices sang
    I listened, listened
    my feet looked outside
    listening, I shut my eyes
    everything was black, I floated

    deep-diamond-blue — falling
    no fear, my mouth opened
    head turned around and around

    eyes bowed, in the divide
    between past and future
    a new cycle had begun

    I would never be the same again

COUNTDOWN

[six]
darkness everywhere
— crying torrents

[five]
someone fell

[four]
scream, wrench open the door
blood glass, wild spikes lodged in wounds

[three]
wailing and kicking
blood poured like a burst egg

[two]
howling secret names, potions
struck words into ears, legs twisting

[one]
loud muddy swamp,
skulls flew

VIOLET DESERT

sandstorms, concealed
mirage cities

phosphorescent figures
innumerable souls

names on the wall of hearts
a sacred grove of empty houses

great wastes
stone carvings of death

INVISIBLE

ghosts thrust up

    from the sand

I fight to escape

    scorching desert vowels pour out

my hair bursts into flames

    bright yellow butterflies from the sun

fly into my mouth

    mysteries of generations

tear from my throat

TORRENT

emptiness swallowed me up
I slept two hundred years
the morning grew afraid,
frightened even the gods
colossal night spaces
yearning like airplanes
our roof slept, wind cracked
above a floor of rain
fantasies dreamt future
white umbrellas, spirit
whispered, expanded
new forces were being born
tigers of the divine
dragons of justice, fierce
force of hurricanes
then silence, a dazzling calm
restored the open air
earth's blood evaporated, wiped dry
a new music flowed down my face
filled me, bright

FREEDOM-WORLD-DREAM-BRAIN

/ you, desolate
cities burn
you, beaten
continue to rebel

      / seek justice
      perform justice
      city, full of justice
      restore justice

            / we had stopped
            paying attention
            mouths spoke of roads
            and consciousness

                  / we went
                  from room to room
                  knocking,
                  waking people up

SUN

hot in the sky
sun made my eyes white
I began to see
how the world is
all things linked
in the same place

2 / SANGUE

our ancestors meet the future of the world.

the rich
eat people up.

IN MEMORIAM

1.

I am trying to learn
how to walk on cement
without disturbing the dead
but my eyes have seen
the way a body looks
against the concrete
a line of children & elders
carrying sodas & snacks
the body collapsed,
unsleeping

2.

bodies witness bodies
lose their sovereignty
on the pavement,
observed by people
who are still learning
how to write and read,
children wondering:
what will it be like
to become an adult?

WHISTLE

it's too late to call off the dogs

the dogs know full well

what the trainers are capable of

AND STILL, WE ARE TRYING — TO DREAM

now that I have done
what I'm supposed to do
written the mayor with the names
and badge numbers
of the assassins, tweeted
emailed, called, circulated
my opinion -- prosecute
to the district attorney,
the senator . . .

we are in mourning.

now that my son
and my daughter
have returned home
and no kkk officers
stopped them en route

now that the mayor
decided he'd better listen
and, no -- it's not enough
to just separate officers
from their employment
after performing
the public lynching

now that the officer
has been suspended for the murder
and I can't-won't-think ahead
that he'll be let off anyway
like the racist beasts
who've pummeled generations

can I now say what is boiling inside me?

I don't want   to write another poem   about murder

senseless,   I already have   too many poems, about

how scared   I am   for the safety   of my son,   my daughter

I cannot write   any more poems   about country,   police, or   klan

assassination or violence   inequality,   dead mote of democracy

or going high   when they   go low

or people dead   in a car   or killed   at their kitchen table

police   are the biggest gang   this world   has ever known

and they   get paid, get   covered and respect

while our children,   and loved ones   are still   hanging

from trees   except   the trees   are gone

and all   the marching   the court cases,   burnt

draft cards,   movements   elections,   running for office

organizing,   buttons,   boycotts   laws,

studies,   chants,   reading   writing,   songs,

music,   films   posters,   the offerings

all   the blood spilt,   just comes   down   to one mf's knee bend

by a car,   slowly   suffocating

a human being   in front of   the whole world

—and nothing!

where is the silence / the / stop !

                                                  the mourning

                                                       the sick
                                                       weary

                                                     feeling
                                                        of
                                                     disgust

                                                       that
                                                    this place

                                                      this
                                                  united states

                                                        is
                                                   the sickest
                                                      place
                                                    on earth

                                                       and
                                                      here
                                                     we are

                                                      still,
                                                     trying
                                                  —to dream

21

DISAMBIGUATION OF
CYBORG TEMPERAMENTS

<p><em

penal code 422 in the pandemic
I don't believe in conspiracy theories
it's just that the police are listening
to our phones and laptops
the only things we have
to communicate
IP address: *freedom%of?speech^

the internet is not my mother
the internet is not my mother, I tell my pulse
the internet is dead!
but even the pictographs of our ancestral DNA
are caught inside its web

WHITE SUPREMACY'S IDENTITY CRISIS
AS SLOW-MOTION-CRASH

- Found poem from cspan reporting on the January 6 insurrection

we brought this hell upon ourselves
it is a wrenching day
our words and actions have had consequences
of a very very negative nature

we ought to watch our words
and think about
what they should mean

attacked by the enemy within
everyone says *we the people*
if those are *the people*
we are in a lot of trouble

justice must not fail
feast on the epiphany

SHADES OF WHITE

- I wrote this after the January 6 insurrection. It is a sequenced list of actual tones of white paint currently sold in the U.S. to coat the walls of homes and buildings. Hegemony is ubiquitous. I sequenced the words ironically to question the qualities assigned whiteness, and added one word: seditious.

capitol white	swiss coffee	oyster white
bone white	parchment	white reflection
pale smoke	white flour	
winter mood	seditious white	extra white
victorian pewter	chantilly lace	casa blanca
silver charm	alabaster	silk white
oatmeal	pure white	antique white
macaroon		aged paper
moth gray	cloud white	lava white
closet mix	moonlight white	white duck
master mix	creamy white	natural choice
	accessible beige	
eggshell white	agreeable gray	best white
powder	alabaster	super white
paper white	diamond muslin	simply white
white dove	seed pearl	extra white
snowfall white	snow bound	halo white

SPRING IN EMPIRE

spring rolled in, uniformed
carrying mace and a pistol
handcuffing children in the snow

spring barged in, guilty.
socks up to its knees
leather belt yanked tight

spring floated on an iceberg
disputing the rationality of public lynchings
flagrant ineptitude of mercy

spring strode in
saying, *this is not who we are*
oh, but it is. it has been

spring arrived in the city
of immoral mortals
white domination's henchmen

spring is under interrogation
it has been detained
by the wretched theater of continuity

plague of titanic proportions
will there be spring this year
or will it remain, merciless winter?

JULY 4 *

dat-tat,

boom
crack crack,   tat-tat-tat

zeeeeeeeeezzz,   crooom-bap

wheerrrrrrrr,   hiiiiirrrrrrr,
boom

paaaaaaaaaaaap
                    paaaaaaaaaaaap

crrrrl,   tat-tat,   booooom
        plat-plat-
flashhhhhhh

                    booooooooooom, tat

bam, bam, pittttt,

pop!

* independence does not mean blowing things up

WE DISSENT

BREYER, SOTOMAYOR, and KAGAN, J.J. dissenting

today's decision is certain: the curtailment of women's rights, and of their status as free and equal citizens.

Constitution will provide no shield, despite its guarantees of liberty and equality for all.

REPETITION

1964 /

I was born into an uprising
gestated inside freedom summer
dad in mississippi, mom in the bronx
she, growing me and raising my sisters
he, looking for goodman, schwerner, and chaney
voter registration workers
buried in a ditch at dusk
rifles clipped inside the cabins
of klan pickup trucks

1992 /

my son was born into an uprising
gestated inside a family
that would've been illegal
apartment in the back
so neighbors wouldn't see us
windows and doors
facing an intersection of alleys
hollering trash

2020 /

this page was born into an uprising
gestated inside a pandemic
no more clutched words, bitten tongues
fear like kindling
hidden in hands behind our backs
children of the dark earth, proceed
latent freedoms are promised
from the past
to the fathomable,
unfathomable now

BOUNTY

two days before his stillness
dad's sunflower body drooped
in a navy blue wheelchair,
he made a declaration

— I apologize, he said to his children
our mother, and a physician
he did this out of responsibility
a warning about unavoidable truth

some exits echo
he knew this from experience
25 years had passed
since his own mother died
died, he preferred not *passed away*

mom's sentences landed on the quiet kitchen table
her hands clasped, *if you do that*
please save me a seat.
first, he said to the clotting quiet
I have to find a seat for myself

two nights later, his breathing stopped
and returned the next morning
in the body of a small black bird
drowning in a pool of water

tsipor! tsipor! my doda cried
I scooped him up with a wad of bounty
rested him inside a makeshift paper towel nest
he shook, fluffed his sleek dark feathers

grandma landed on the roof, calling to him
he wattled in a circle
and off they flew, skyward

dad was an atheist
and I don't believe in reincarnation
I'm just stating the facts
and have a photograph to prove it

(I want   to write my father   but if I do,

more of him   might   evaporate

he might   be   more gone.   maybe if i don't

try.   to write my father,   I'll remember)

NENÊM

nenêm, nicknamed for baby, my eldest nephew
never left the body of a boy
nenêm, nickname shared with a dona. todos podem ser nenês
meninos o meninas, modernos o velhinhas
I remember you in shorts, chapeu, chinelo
brincando wheelbarrow streets of bonfim. maracujá, limão, pão
fazendo mandados para os adultos, changing long-necked
empty bottles into cerveja, coca, guaraná
our rowboat adventures, navegando the flat mar salgado
you, balancing a wooden vessel filled with children
two bodies ahead e dois atrás, eu no meio pra equilibrar
crab traps bigger than our arms or spindly legs
lembro de você — before the loaf of bread, the bed, the bullet
silhouetted against the vast atlantic, flipping upside down into the sky

THE FUTURE OF MUSIC

"I was just going home. I have no gun. I don't even kill flies."
— Elijah McClain

> >

a siren lights the sky
its howl, a chant
flaming darkness

on the street, beside
a police car, a needle
makes an injection

the spirit of a violinist
in orange sneakers, bellows
truth falls from his face
like broken teeth

the world stops its breath

> >

the mother prays
for angel wings
and naked feet
to lift his weight

baby, she sang
when he was born
praying over his limbs
and stalk, his certainty

elijah singing, elijah
playing, praising
dancing, elijah
his cup filled to the brim

a son who serenades
cats in their cages
his bow, reverberating string

the mother sings
baby, you are a soul
and this is
a spiritual revolution

> >

I know a psalm when I hear one
when you murder the future of music
you are conjuring extinction

revenge made of roses
and umbilical cords

> >

children of the police officers
at home in their beds, sleeping
tomorrow would be their summer

the man who washes patrol cars
will scrub the declarations
of a 23 year old from the bumper
with a thick yellow sponge
frothing soapy water

> >

parents hide their children
like acorns in their cheeks
to keep them safe for winter

we march, to a public
recitation of names
not just the panopticon
of lives, but its thievery

the world goes
to demonstrations
wearing masks

the masks, folded
and thin, accumulate
cellular matter,
the virus says not a word
the virus speechless, like the mothers
antennae tuned to murder

> >

I envy the dead,
not because I want to go
but because their witnessing is different
who can be witness
to these times
and not want to be thunder?

thunder,
skipping off
into   the distance
cautiously   shaking

    venus

  pluto

        mars

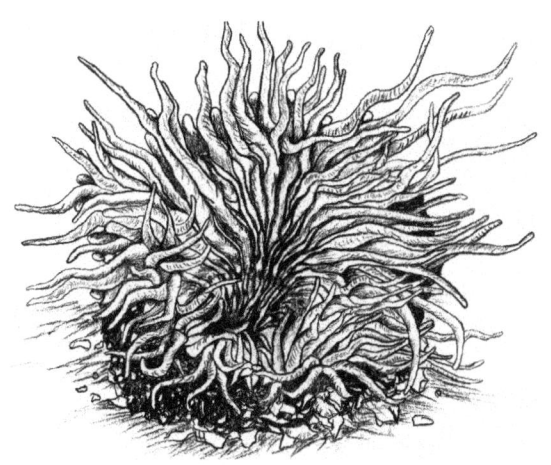

3 / PELAGE

when it comes to violence,
you can't out violence the monster

DIRGE

- after Rabindranath Tagore

he has made
his ignorance a crown,
& the flesh of the earth
a mortuary

our species
digs and digs
its own grave.

STOP A WAR

"I don't understand why people keep choosing fascism."
— my mother

my words are knots,
        while I need parachutes.
sleepless from threading imaginary strategies
        potential sentences to disrupt the violence.
try lots of periods . . . .
        put the [killers in brackets]

some writers spin enviable lines,
        bumper sticker responses at the ready
then go out for cappuccino.
        as if the correct terminology
could bring back the dead

my body can't sleep
        for grieving
head shakes remembering
        do Nascimento's lyric:
eu sou america do sul,
        eu sei você não vai saber.

same with everywhere,
        imperial windows can't see in
much less out.
        do something, her body said

the world is on fire
you can only change
           what you touch
how can a mom
           bring down a fascist state?
massage therapists post information
           on demonstrations
they sing, bring flowers
           and are dragged on the ground by police
fascism comes in all flavors
           styles and sizes
anyone can be a fascist
           two for one — on sale now

maybe anyone can be
           a freedom fighter too,
I want to stop the war
           words made the world
but mine roar within
           I misspell lines, small lions

the people who are doing the fighting
           are the ones who must stop.
I want to make them
           let's see, I have hot water
and a barrel of lemons
           try! use your words!
stop a war with your body

we are not all that powerful, h says
           it's ok. we are not built for that.
but my body of moon dust
           cells & pillage histories
dreams of becoming
           big as a u.n.
an i.c.c.
           BIGGER!

a small body
        dreams of being
a body of power

        but she is more
like a garden bird
        small and two-footed,
feathered with emotion
        while history wears
boots and helmets
        carries rifles, barges in
drops bombs and burns

we will get crushed
        if we try to carry the world, h says
but that is what
        the body feels responsible for

how does a mother stop a war?
        the people who are bombing must stop
the mother stirs,
        but we must find a way
to stop them.

ARTIFACTS OF DISASTER

"israel is an artifact of anti-seminism."

— *fred moten*

/
the state is an artifact of exclusion
the military is an artifact of sorrow
the body is a fact

children are the artifacts of families
communities, the artifacts of forestation
bombs are also facts

the present is an artifact of depravity
the past, an artifact of curatorial power
the future: tbd

/
ima sheli's first
non-perishable acquisition
was a pair of silver earrings
stamped in english
made in palestine

/
my uncle liked to tell me stories
about his mischievous sister
ima ran under camels
following a neighbor's finger
disappeared down the road,
he was sent to find her
and wouldn't trade her for goats

/
now, the husbands are dead
the brothers, the sisters in law
of course, the parents
and the grandparents

/
two sisters still live
on two sides of an ocean
doda says, *why does your mother
let politics divide us?*

/
i'll never go back, ima says
until they change their politics

/
a crisis that never ends
must end, must
why can't people
imagine
something
else?

CEASE FIRE . ALTO AL FUEGO . CESSAR FOGO

I woke from sleep
as if an earthquake
shook the curve
of our planet without sides
deafening quiet
the sound of a cease-fire

me desperté del sueño
como si un terremoto
sacudiera la curva
de nuestro planeta sin lados
silencio ensordecedor
el sonido de un alto el fuego

eu acordei do sono
como se um terremoto
sacudir a curva
do nosso planeta sem lados
calma ensurdecedor
o som de um cessar-fogo

CONSIDERING WAR

- after Cesar Vallejo's "considerando el frío, imparcialmente" & the bombing of Kherson where my paternal grandmother was born and fled from in the Pale of Settlement.

considering that bombs
        leave craters in the earth
        making it difficult
        to mobilize hospitals,
        carry pregnant mothers
        across fields of rubble

comprehending the cold breath of sunday
        broken bridges
        families gathered beneath them
        without exact destinations
        beyond a border

understanding that mammals with bombs
        are cold hearted
        explosive-death-machines

considering that tyrants
        —and I will call them that
        because of their bombs —
        explode sites
        leaving the enduring silence
        of family members

understanding that a cadaver
      cannot speak

& I am just a storyteller
      still living
      with the possibility of voice

I will make my breath a sign
      painted in horror
      across the sky
      that begs the bombing
      to stop

I HELD THE WAR

inside my body
suffocating,
head pulled down
into the rubble

now, I am longing
for the olive tree warbler to return
jerusalem sage, tall as children

TZIDUR / A NEW BOOK COULD BE WRITTEN

no calm or peace or future
will ever come from denying people a sense of home

no story of home
has the right to obliterate all other stories of home

home is shaped
by the stories people tell about the land

stories are
made up things made real on the land

some stories
clobber other stories; they aim to obliterate

hold up a mirror to militarism
may the bloody generations of outsidering

end
with us

CATASTROPHIC MOLTING

I moisten my body with oil
remove all armaments & mementos
shave the head with a knife
step away from expectation
list making, comparisons
& my very own personal death threats
everything was taken from me but my doubt
even that is finally becoming dust

pass the defense field of cactus flowers,
the primus gas stove
meet yourself in a doorway at midnight
bring the book of songs
from the back of your brain
written in the languages
you weren't permitted to know

this-is-the-story:

      in a hole underground
      there is a stone above your solar plexus
      above that, a mat
      above that, an animal
      above that, a feather
      above that, a fly

I was told this, to reject the ditch

notice, the small buzzing insect
is the only creature with enough courage
to make the offering
& turn shit into fertilizer

I set out,
inside my bundle
was a pair of eyes
determined to read the sky
for its sun

in between the space of knowing
and not knowing is infinity
all I want to know now
is how   not   to be caught

seek harmony with knowing
find elation in the listening

& when it is my turn
because   everything has one

I will blow tsunami-wind
to rattle clear the desks

I am writing & reading at the same time

rowing   to create a rhythm

eyes set   on the river

sunlight glittering   as it does when it is seen

turns out

there is no way   to go nowhere

it's impossible

to do nothing

stepping off   might actually be   stepping in

turning away   might actually be   turning toward

what would happen
if there was no time,
no hatchet, no erasure
what if were a part of a whole
that loved us without ceasing?

NEW MOON IN CANCER

let us dream again, or for the very first time
as if the winds wanted it so, and were on our side
as if today was now, and we were able

hear the clicking song of finches
hold your feathered self
in your own peace of mind
make a wish for something true that matters

begin right here right now
with your own two lips, breath and hands
wanting and knowing how to be

OUR FOREMOTHERS GREET THE UNBORN

write a woman
digging holes for ghosts,
raging through the ruins

write her made of milk
the cells of her body
creamy sweet

write her pounding earth
move along the fractures
red-eyed, saltwater cheeks

write her seeing beyond the burning
betrothed to a story
that doesn't wish us dead

write her seated on a mat
communing with the divine
worlds resting on her lap

write her wrist, copper-bangled
brass bell clutched in her hand
ring/ing, ring/ing, ring/ing, ring/ing
ring/ing, ring/ing, ring/ing, ring/ing

AFTERWORD

Poetry shows up in my life as a divining rod and outlet. When I am frustrated or afraid, poetry is honest and courageous. I've come to believe that poetry can help us practice our best virtues and change culture for the better.

The poems in this book open with a rupture. I became ill early in the pandemic, before a vaccine had been developed or much was known about COVID-19. I couldn't speak, and I wasn't sure if this would be the end of my life. I became obsessed with making erasure poems, marking up xeroxed sheets from Ben Okri's 1991 novel *The Famished Road*, a book that I'd been taking refuge in. The creative process of recovery was documented in two interviews that are available online: one with *Capsule Stories* and another with BBC Radio. The erasures became a limited edition chapbook *Endless Bowls of Sky* (Placeholder Press, 2020). This allowed me to give voice to my fears and the healing process.

Another pivotal moment was writing the poem in this collection "And Still, We Are Trying — to Dream." The poem taught me an important life lesson. Not only can anger be non-harming, it can potentially reduce future harm. Writing poems against violence is a way to reject dehumanizing behavior, and systems, while inspiring empathy for change.

I was in a writer's circle the day after Mr. Floyd was murdered by Derek Chauvin.

"You sound angry," my elder said.

"I am." I wept with frustration. "Furious."

As a mother and a teacher, I didn't believe that I was entitled to my rage. Hope was my profession and responsibility. But there it was: anger, eating me up.

"Write your anger."

I stayed up all night filling pages with scribbles and markings.

The next morning, I went to see my son, a musician, and we recorded it in his living room. I sent the audio file to friends, who shared it with their own circles. It was picked up for publication by *ArtPlace America* and inspired a public art exhibition in Cary, North Carolina. The poem touched people all over the country who I had never met. Lots of people were frustrated and angry too.

The challenges have kept coming. We are witnessing senseless violence, mass shootings, the threat of climate collapse, rampant corruption, and the dissolution of legislation aiming to protect the most vulnerable including the Voting Rights Act (1965) and Roe v. Wade (1973). We dissent!

Facing these times has been accompanied by a heightened awareness of who I am, what I come from, what I believe in, and who I love. Here we are, living and writing through these times. Racism, xenophobia, and patriarchy have always been a part of my family story — the scariest parts. I don't want the persistence of violence to cannibalize our futures. An important aim of my work as a culture maker is to imagine and cogenerate futures.

Gracias to Flowersong Press for giving this collection a home. Special thanks to Edward Vidaurre, Lina Suarez, and Jo Reyes-Boitel at Flowersong. Kudos to Miyo Stevens-Gandara for her attention to the butterfly eyelashes of her imagination on the cover art. Gratitude to Gayle Brandeis for her fabulosity, mentorship, and example. Thanks Leonora Simonovis, Adrian Ernesto Cepeda, Karen Llagas, Yeva Johnson, Lydia T. Liu, Theri Pickens, Rachel Myers, Angela Siew, Deena Metzger, Sabata-mpho Mokae, Mamle Kabu, Carlos Moore, Valecia Phillips, Genevieve Kaplan, Delia Xóchitl Chavez, Ife Williams, A.H. Jerriod Avant, A'bena Awuku-Larbi, Epifania Akosua Amoo-Adare, Katleho Kano, Ana Rita Santiago, Glenis Redmond, Jenise Miller, Gloria Carrera, Margarita de León, Nana Asaase, Martin Egblewogbe, Teio Xaggat, Efe Paul Azino, Michaela Paulette Shirley, Atlas Theo Chester Shirley, Yonatan Perry, Antioch University Creative Writing Program, Community of Writers, Writer's Project Ghana, Lagos International Poetry Festival, East 64th, Women Who Submit, Self Help Graphics and Art, Brasil Brasil Cultural Center, and Orunmila Afedefeyo. With gratitude for my ancestors, mishpucha, familia, and communities. For Avila and Reva, everything. I am grateful for the opportunity to write and be read, speak and be heard, listen and keep learning.

ACKNOWLEDGMENTS

I gratefully acknowledge the editors and curators who first welcomed poems from this book into their journals, anthologies, and exhibitions.

ArtPlace America: "and still, we are trying —to dream." Special thanks to Michaela Paulette Shirley.

BOOM California (edited by Romeo Guzman): "shades of white," "white supremacy's identity crisis as a slow motion crash"

Capsule Stories Special Isolation Series (edited by Carolina Von Kampen): "endless bowls of sky"

Clarendon House Books (*Poetica: Inner Circle Poetry Group Writer's Anthology of Poetry 2019):* "single motherhood is a party"

Community of Writers, Written Here and There: "bounty"

New Verse News: "stop a war" & "considering war"

Placeholder Press: "endless bowls of sky," "10 nights," "countdown," "violet desert," "invisible," "torrent," "freedom-world-dream-brain," "sun."

Prairie Schooner (edited by Mahtem Shiferraw and Kwame Dawes. Special thanks to Neela Banerjee): "the future of music"

Self Help Graphics & Art, "cease fire. alto al fuego. cessar fogo" *Everything Connected: Land, Body, Cosmos,* curated by Miyo Stevens Gandara. The work was displayed in the center, published in the exhibition catalog, and archived online by *Google Arts & Culture.*

Town of Cary, North Carolina: "and still, we are trying —to dream" and "in memoriam" catalyzed the exhibition *We Must Look and Reflect to Make Change Happen* curated by Denise Dickens.

FINGERPRINT OF HISTORY
Author Interview with Diane Gottlieb

Diane: Congratulations on your new collection *Catastrophic Molting*. It rocked me! Here are a few words I wrote down to describe how I feel about your poems: Fierce, bold. Wise, unflinching. Tender, mama bear, badass, loving, hopeful. Fearless.

And when I say fearless, I don't mean you have no fear, but that you do and say what you have to do and say regardless of fear.

Amy: Coming from an activist, immigrant family I always asked myself the questions: how will you support your family, and how will you make a difference in the world? My origins are 99.9% Ashkenazi. Whatever you have to say about the Jewish diaspora, there's no denying that a lot of effort has gone into trying to exterminate us. Many vulnerable communities experience the repercussions of fear or shaming. If you are not careful, it can turn into self loathing.

If there is a way to step into a fearless type of life, poetry has been my guide. There is a mystery to poetry, and I am devoted to it partly because of the energy it brings me. It's a no-BS way of writing. I don't think I could have created the changes in my life I've been striving for without it. It was the perfect medium, the great companion.

Diane: How did you come to poetry?

Amy: I've always written with line breaks. Even when I was a girl. I journaled and was lucky to have two teachers who let me respond in poetry to some of the assignments.

I read a lot of poetry in Spanish as a young woman. I spent a good deal of time in Mexico, in Nicaragua, and later in Brazil. I would read poetry in Spanish out loud, and sing in Portuguese and a bit of Yoruba, while I was trying to learn the languages.

I speak Spanish, I speak Portuguese, I play capoeira. I spent almost as much time immersed in Afro-Brazilian culture as I did in my parents home. No matter how much you learn from your loved ones, it's important to know and value your own heritage. But I did not learn my mother tongues Hebrew and Yiddish— yet. I'm beginning to humbly study the aleph bet. Every letter has significance. The Kabbalah's Sephirot (תּוֹרִיפַס) suggests that knowledge is based on intimacy. You can't know anything as a stranger. When we ask questions (המכח), develop a devoted practice (הניב), and make sense of things in an embodied way (תעד) we are creating our lives, ourselves, and our relations.

Diane: How would you feel when people call you a political or feminist poet? Do you see yourself as those?

Amy: Jose Louis Borges's idea that metaphor is two things brought together helps me imagine my identities. I am a constellation of metaphors, of things brought together. My origins are Ashkenasi. We came to the U.S. via Jerusalem, and from shtetls in Pitkamien, Kherson, and Kalisz. But life and my family are more expansive than one cultural experience. My children are Jewish, Ifa, Middle Eastern, North and South American, Black, Afro-descendant Brazilian. We're spiritual people, interfaith, multicultural, and multinational. This is family, this is our love, this is our flesh.

Am I a womanist or an intersectional feminist? Absolutely, how couldn't you be? Half the population is female. We're the reproducers of our species, and yet we're treated as if we don't have even basic rights over our own physiology.

I have to be anti-racist because I am not an idiot. Our family has been on the other side of fascism, xenophobia, and hatred. I don't have the luxury of taking a back seat on that because this is me and this is my family, my own heritage and our own futures. But does the United States have a good tag for me? No. They wanted us to assimilate, to disappear and forget. But I come from an ancient culture and language. I'm in the process of restoration thanks to polylingual writer friends Mamle Wolo, Sabata-mpho Mokae, Gloria Carrera, Margarita Leon, Eleuterio Exaggat, and Rabbi Yonatan Perry.

It's not because I want to be hard to understand, but I do want to be authentic, so I see myself as the constellation of metaphors.

Diane: You go to the hard places, the places that hurt. Sometimes the ugly places. What does putting words to that do for you?

Amy: It's funny, I really don't want to go to the ugly places, and or be particularly political. I want to be one who brings hope. I want to be one who brings sunshine. I want to bring love and understanding. But when I sit on the page, I just have to obey. These poems are what needed to be said.

Diane: You go there, but your poems are not ugly. They're truth—your truth and so many others.' And they're very hopeful. You take hard topics and squeeze out hope. You find it.

Amy: Well, hope is necessary. I don't "try" to have hope. It's my job as a mother, as a teacher. We do not have the luxury to drop our hands and say to the next generation, "There is no hope." That's not a possibility. But the future demands honesty. Honesty and action.

Poetry gives me a productive way to put all those feelings down and work with them. To wash them, to put my hands in them. To weave with them. I'm putting them in a river of language, and I'm washing them in the water with my hands and trying to weave something new from what is there.

Diane: You write about things going on in the larger world, but you also write about the personal. Do you feel that when you write, you're healing yourself?

Amy: Absolutely. I was very hesitant to write about patriarchy in a personal way, publicly in the sphere of family. I guess it makes no sense. So many people have experienced difficult moments in their relationships that led to suffering. I shouldn't be embarrassed to write about any of that. One of the healing processes for a post-divorce family that's changing is to continue to heal the relationships. I can say that I have an excellent relationship with my ex-husband now, and even with his second wife. There's a lot of mutual respect. Children deserve to not feel divided, and everyone has healing to do. It's always easy to point to the person who's hurt you and say, "They harmed me, they're the bad one." We get to evolve.

However, I do feel that single mothers in particular bear the brunt of so much patriarchy. For example, the current political discussions about the value and rights of the fetus. Fine. But once the fetus becomes a child and is out in the world, there is not an equal commitment to caring for that household, that mother and that child. Where is that support? Where is the ferocity of people in the streets to support actual families who've been through some kind of trauma, or who have taken on a lot for one person to hold?

I do speak out very clearly against patriarchy. That does not mean speaking out against men. It means speaking out against the way cultures and societies are formed to render women invisible. Desechable, or disposable. The work mothers do— especially single mothers — is so critical, and I don't see the support.

Diane: Let's talk about your collection *Catastrophic Molting*.

Amy: I'm happy that this book found a home with the wonderful FlowerSong Press. Initially, there was another book that the manuscript was attached to. I separated the work into two collections because of vision and length. Part of me wanted to just leapfrog over this book, and jump to the nature and languages oriented book. I had to force myself not to do that and to just be in those difficult feelings.

Its hard to write about a moment which was absolutely true, and then it takes another year or two to get it ready for publication and out into bookstores and online. By time, you've already evolved into a new state of mind. There is a gap, rhythmically, between the creation of work, the circulation of work, and the next thing you're learning.

Because of the gravity of the pandemic, and what people have called the racial reckoning, the suffering has been so deep, that I felt mixed feelings about bringing readers back to where we were. On the other hand, I know it should be recorded, and it's okay to have it be recorded in different people's voices, including my own. If I take a longer cosmological view, I think *just let it be.*

Diane: I love what you wrote about anger in the afterword to the book.

Amy: I don't like to feel angry. When I feel angry, I struggle with what to do with that feeling. It's so hard. I've learned to make a date with your sadness, be in the feeling. It takes so much work to try to not feel what you actually feel. It's better just to feel it, be in it, let it flow through you, and be ready and open for the next feeling.

After Derek Chauvin murdered George Floyd, I was just so furious, so sick to my stomach. As a Jewish person, I've always thought, how did the people living in Europe let the Shoah happen? How did they let the extermination camps happen right in front of their faces? I don't want to be a hypocrite. If I'm alive at this time, and I see this happening to people, I have to say something.

Writing my anger was a way for me to not be silent in the face of that kind of violence. I'm not a Senator, I'm not the President, I'm not a congressperson. I'm a mom and a teacher. A person. I'm alive. I'm a poet, so let me say something through poetry. That's how this whole book was made. How can I speak back, or speak to these times with my voice?

Writing your anger can actually draw a boundary to say, "No. This kind of behavior is not okay with us." Theoretically, it could prevent future harm. Poetry is one of the ways to be non-harming, and hopefully to create greater empathy.

Diane: Your go-to is poetry, but you also write essays?

Amy: Yes. I write essays. I've also edited books of prose, and worked on documentary treatments. My first published writing were academic essays about feminist discussions of community, place, and education. Poetry feels the most intimate to me. It's my autochthonous tongue. I respect what it can do and where it wants to go. Writing poetry feeds a particular part of me that is subterranean. It is also good for me, and, hopefully, for readers too. Poetry is medicinal.

Diane: Can you tell us a little bit about the title of your poem "Catastrophic Molting"?

Amy: Catastrophic molting is a scientific term. This is the story. We had been quarantining for a year and a half or so by then, and my children and my son's partner decided it was time to get out. We borrowed a car and drove up the coast. On the way, we saw this beach of sea lions resting on the sand. Thousands and thousands and thousands of sea lions resting on the sand. They lay there, using their bodies to flip sand onto their backs. They bark, they sleep. I thought, oh, well that's what being in quarantine feels like. They rest, they make an agreement to be non-violent with each other while they are in a vulnerable state. I was fascinated by resting as transformative social action, like the Nap Ministry.

I also was moved by the state of losing your skin and growing new fur. That is what the pandemic experience has been for me, a total transformation of my biology and my life. I think a lot of people feel similarly. It is about the energy of the word. "Catastrophic" obviously sounds difficult, but "molting" is about renewal.

Diane: Many of your poems are about renewal. For example, "The Future of Music."

Amy: Oh my gosh, that poem was just... I was so furious and heartbroken. As a mother of Black children, I had to write. I didn't necessarily think I would share it with anyone. Neela Banerjee asked me to submit poems to a colleague of hers at Prairie Schooner. Mahtem Shiferraw chose to publish the poem in a series she co-edited by Kwame Dawes. When two phenomenal writers and editors say this poem needs to be shared, I will accept that.

Diane: You're very versatile, also. I love "July 4th". It's just all these sounds of firecrackers, bouncing around the page amidst white space, and then there's a little asterisk at the bottom": "independence does not mean blowing things up." You have these short, little beauties that just say it all, like "Whistle": "It's too late to call off the dogs. The dogs know full well what the trainers are capable of." What more is there to say about that? And then there are poems that are all hope, like "New Moon and Cancer."

Amy: So how do you end a book? Because this book is hard and painful, I felt worried about leaving readers at that emotional beat. For a while, the manuscript concluded on the poem "Catastrophic Molting" which ends with the question: "what if we were a part of a whole that loved us without ceasing?"

What if we didn't have to always live on the defensive? What if we could just be? What if we moved with a deep cosmographic awareness of our interdependence? I added "New Moon and Cancer" and "Our Foremothers Greet the Unborn" to end the book because the poems start to move forward with that understanding. What if we were a part of a whole that loved us without ceasing? It's the question of life.

What if we were to hold ourselves with that tremendous care, and believe that possibility was on our side? "New Moon and Cancer" goes back to the qualities of mindfulness. Let us breathe, and let us be in our deeper knowing, and let us greet each other in that way. The answer to society's ills will not come from the perfect hashtag or policy. It will come from social movements and policies, but also from how we behave as human beings on earth now. Those are the stories I want to tell.

Diane: Can you speak about what you are writing next?

Amy: The next book is about grounding in the natural world. In the face of climate collapse, it's unabashedly multilingual. It leaps off of English, Spanish, Hebrew and Portuguese. One of the poems is an entire section that's translated by my friends into their other languages including Twi, Otomi, Mazateco, and Tagalog. It moves from this period of trauma to focus on the natural world with a devotion and adoration for the multiplicity of mother tongues and languages. Beneath the poems is a search for decarbonization, decolonization, and global connection.

A lot of the words are trite by now: Solidarity, brotherhood, sisterhood. They don't really capture it. It's the reality, it's the cosmographic reality of our existence. That's where I'm headed. But out of respect, perhaps for the dead or for those who have suffered or are still suffering in their own ways, I'm allowing *Catastrophic Molting* to come out and speak to that moment as a fingerprint of history.

ABOUT THE TITLE

Catastrophic Molting is the collective ritual of loss and regeneration experienced by sea elephants (Mirounga Angustirostris) along the California coast. While molting, the mirounga rest together on the shore, and fast to preserve their energy. Collective resting provides social protection during times when they are most vulnerable. Only through these periods of dramatic change can they grow sleek new coats.

ABOUT THE AUTHOR

Amy Shimshon-Santo is a writer and educator who believes that creativity is a powerful tool for personal and social transformation. She is the author of *Even the Milky Way is Undocumented* (Unsoliticed Press), *Endless Bowls of Sky* (Placeholder Press), and numerous peer-reviewed essays (*GeoHumanities*; *Education, Citizenship, and Social Justice*; *PUBLIC, Entropy*, among others). Her writing has appeared in *Prairie Schooner, ArtPlace America, Zócalo Public Square, Entropy, Journal of Writers Project Ghana, Tilt West, Boom CA, Yes Poetry, SUNY Press, Public*, and Google Arts & Culture, among others. She has been nominated for three Pushcart Prizes in poetry and creative nonfiction, a Rainbow Reads Award, an Emmy Award and LA Press Award (*Arts Education*, KCET / PBS SoCal), and was a finalist for the Nightboat Book Poetry Prize. Amy has edited two books amplifying community voices: *Et Al: New Voices in Arts Management* (Illinois Open Publishing Network, and *Arts = Education* (UC Press). Amy began her creative career in dance, performance, and capoeira, and continues to move across geographies and disciplines. Her teaching career has spanned research universities, community centers, K-12 schools, arts organizations, and spaces of incarceration. www.amyshimshon.com

ABOUT THE COVER ARTIST

Miyo Stevens-Gandara is a Los Angeles based artist working in a variety of media which include photography, drawing, embroidery, and various printmaking mediums. Her imagery explores issues of ancestry, migration, feminism, cultural identity, and environmental degradation. She received her BFA from the California College of the Arts, and her MFA from the California Institute of the Arts. Her work is in the collections of the Los Angeles County Museum of Art, Museum of Latin American Art (MoLAA) Riverside Art Museum, and private collections. Her work has been exhibited in the U.S. and internationally. Miyo has a strong commitment to her community as part of her art practice throughout her career, and in her role as a tenured Assistant Professor of Photography at Rio Hondo College. www.miyofineart.com.

ABOUT FLOWERSONG PRESS

FLOWERSONG
PRESS

FlowerSong Press nurtures essential verse from, about, and through the borderlands. The voices of those from Latin America, the U.S.A. and all over the world. Literary, lyrical, and boundless, and welcomes allies that understand and join in the voice of people of color and our struggle, truth, and hope. FlowerSong Press publishes novice, emerging, and established writers of poetry, fiction, non-fiction, and children´s books. www.flowersongpress.com